Here is a Christmas market in Germany.
There are all kinds of toys.
Children love to visit the market.

1

These men are making wooden toys.
One man carves the wood.
Another paints the toy.
They have just made a wooden bear.

This man makes violins.
He carves from wood.
He glues the pieces together.
Then he fixes four strings.

Germans love to go to the opera.
An opera is a kind of play.
People sing the words.
An orchestra plays the music.
4

This is a special play about Jesus.
It is acted once every ten years.
All the actors come from the village
of Oberammergau.

Here is a sausage shop.
There are all kinds of sausages.
Some are very spicy.
The boy is buying frankfurters.

Beer festivals are fun.
The people dress up.
Some sing loudly.
Everybody drinks beer.

barley

hops

sugar

yeast

water

1 ingredients

2 boiling

3 fermenting

4 bottling

Beer is made from hops and malt.
The beer is mixed in huge tanks.
Then it is put in vats for weeks.

8

These people are at a carnival.
They dress up for the parade.
There is a parade like this
every year in some towns.

conveyor belt

German cameras are very good.
They have a lot of parts.
These women
are testing all the parts.
10

china figures

kiln

Here are some china figures.
China is made from clay.
The man puts them into the kiln.
The clay shapes are baked in the kiln.

These men are making cars.
These cars are called Volkswagens.
But some people call them beetles.

12

Germany has many long motorways.
There are motorways
in most countries today.
But Germany built the first.

13

launch

tourist boat

There are many castles
along the River Rhine.
Some boats take tourists
to see the castles.
14

barge

Other boats use the Rhine too.
Some barges carry coal.
Other boats carry beer to the towns.

These statues are in a park.
They tell the story
of Hansel and Gretel.
It is an old German fairy tale.

This is the story
of the Pied Piper of Hamelin.
People act the story every year.

sprinter

footballer

diver

gymnast

weight-lifter

Here is a big sports ground.
It has room for many kinds of games.
There are seats for thousands of people.

18

Olympic village

stadium

This was built for the Olympic Games.
Sportsmen come from many countries
to take part in these Games.

Germany long ago

Long ago these men printed a book.
They printed it
on the first printing press.
It was built in Germany.

These men gave a concert.
They played for a prince.
Composers often wrote music
specially for princes.

Here is Carl Benz.
He made the first car.
It could only go slowly.

cabin for passengers

An airship is like a huge balloon.
Airships can fly a long way.
Many people travelled in one like this.
People may travel in airships again.

23

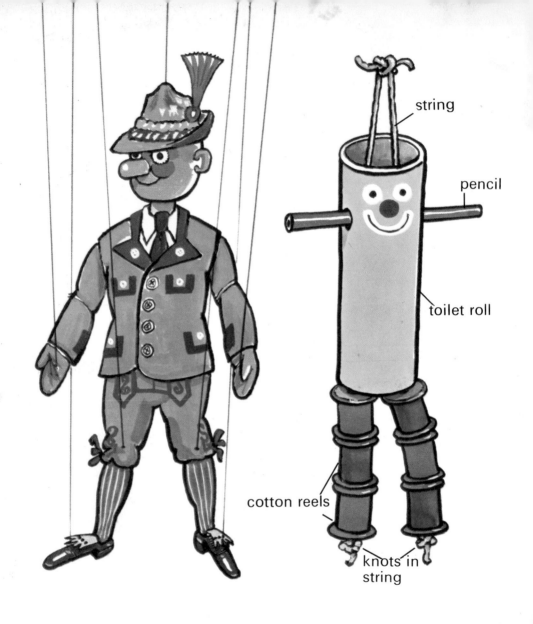

string

pencil

toilet roll

cotton reels

knots in
string

Many puppets are made in Germany.
See if you can make one for yourself.

Starter's **German** words

I	is	ich
you	is	du
yes	is	ja
no	is	nein
good	is	gut
bad	is	schlecht
friend	is	Freund
hello	is	hallo
goodbye	is	auf Wiedersehen
I eat	is	ich esse
I play	is	ich spiele
I swim	is	ich schwimme

Here are some easy German words.
They will help you to make friends
in Germany.

Index